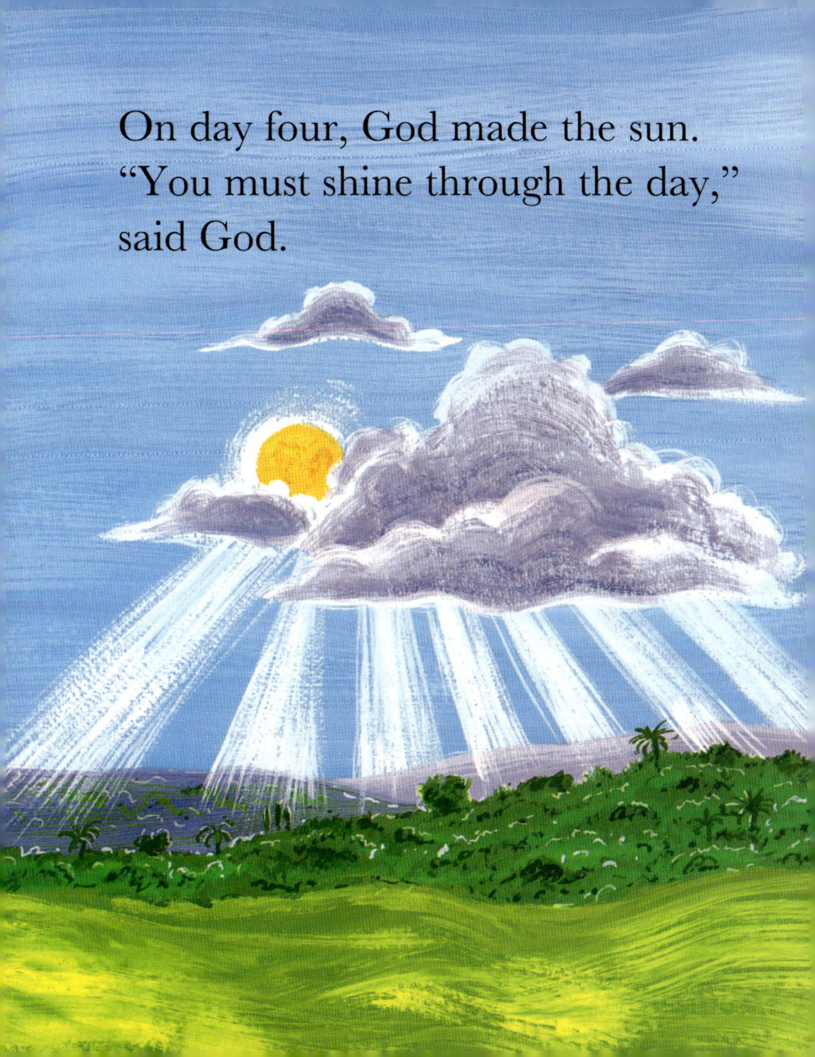

God Makes the World

This

Bible Story Time book

belongs to

____

____

____

Text by Sophie Piper

Published by
Lion Hudson Limited
Wilkinson House, Jordan Hill Business Park,
Banbury Road, Oxford OX2 8DR, England
www.lionhudson.com

ISBN 978 0 7459 6354 9
e-ISBN 978 0 7459 6807 0
ISBN 978 0 7459 7850 5 (pack of 10)

First edition 2005
This edition 2014

A catalogue record for this book is available from the British Library

Printed and bound in China, April 2019, LH54

Bible Story Time

God Makes the World

Sophie Piper * Estelle Corke

LION CHILDREN'S

Imagine a dark and stormy night.

Imagine a dark and stormy sea.

Before the world began, there was only darkness and storm.

Then God spoke: "Let there be light."

The light shone. God had made the very first day.

On the second day, God spoke again: "Let there be sky above and sea below." And there was.

"Next," said God, "I want land as well as sea."

At once the land appeared. Plants began to grow: some were tiny; some were tall.

"I have worked for three days, and everything is very good," said God.

On day four, God made the sun.
"You must shine through the day,"
said God.

"Moon and the stars: I want you to shine at night."

The whole universe did what God commanded.

Early on the fifth morning, God made all kinds of sea creatures: they came darting and diving through the waves.

Then God made the birds. They flapped and flew in the clear air.

On the sixth day, God made the animals – all kinds of amazing animals.

"And last," said God, "I shall make human beings. They will take care of my world."

The six days of making were over.
It was time for a day of rest.

The first man was named Adam. The first woman was named Eve. God gave them a garden home.

"Everything is for you," said God. "There is just one tree you must not touch. If you eat its fruit, everything will go wrong."

Adam and Eve were happy in their paradise home.

One day, a snake came and spoke to Eve. "Did God say you mustn't eat the fruit here?" it asked.

"Only the fruit from one tree," replied Eve. "If we eat that, everything will go wrong."

The snake twisted and wriggled. "Not true!" it said. "The fruit will make you as wise as God. Go on. Try it!"

Eve reached up. She picked the forbidden fruit. She ate some.

"It's good," she said. "I shall give some to Adam."

Adam took a bite. Then he and Eve looked at each other.

"Oh dear," they cried.

"We're both naked," said Eve.

"And now, for the first time, that doesn't seem right," said Adam.

They spent the day making clothes from leaves. Then they heard God coming. They hid among the trees.

God called them.

God found them.

God saw what had happened, and God was sad.

"Now everything must change," said God. "You must say goodbye to paradise. You must go out into the wide world. There you will work for all the things you need."

God made Adam and Eve clothes to wear.

Sadly they walked out of the garden.

As they looked back, they saw an angel with a sword. The blade flashed this way and that. They could not go to the garden ever again.

They looked ahead. “There are lots of weeds here,” said Adam. “But if we work hard, we can plant crops. We’ll manage.”

Eve wiped away a tear. “It’s sad not being friends with God,” she said. “I hope this mistake is put right one day.”